Light
and
the Light

(2007)

*

essay

*

Traumear

*

If we take the light by which we see too much for granted, we may find ourselves lost in the dark, so that we may learn to value it properly. Wisdom arrives with a lamp and teaches us to restore within ourselves the sense of wonder we possessed as children. Our body and mind as one again, not separate as in terms of materialism and spiritualism, respectively, allows us then to perceive beings and world rather than things and the world of things.

*

Light and the Light

From the distinction between light and the light we may extrapolate vision and the formidable apparatus of our senses. Light is pervasive and all that exists does so in light. Knowledge and understanding cannot possibly proceed without light, so that we may simply interchange light and reason when we speak of reality and stand in wonder of the world.

As soon as we speak of 'the' light however, such as when we say: 'He has seen the light', we take into account the universal presence of something, rather than its cosmic or world existence. More precisely, when light is universally present, we call it the light and when the light exists as world we call it light. It is therefore not as if something, who knows what, is present as *the light* or exists as *light*.

What is this third thing, people will say, that either exists as light or is present as the light? However light and the light are not two things. They are not two anything, therefore no third thing can even be imagined that 'brings them forth' or 'in which they reside'. No, there is light and the light and the two are one.

*

The light is initially found within us. Those who find it are said to be enlightened. They look for it because the light within them urges them to do so. It does not cause them to do so, it simply urges. Those who feel urged to do so are pursued by a persistent and distinct *restlessness*.

1

They will not know what this restlessness is about until someone explains it to them or interprets it for them. Then it is entirely up to them whether they commence with this crucial search or not. If they do not, the restlessness may eventually pass and that particular opportunity for enlightenment will have been lost. There may be many more.

The light in its capacity for universal presence is responsible for all that appears. Appearance is a function of the light. Whatever appears is present to our senses. Initially that which truly appears is present to our *sense of wonder*. This sense is the one on which all other senses are based. In other words, if we see but our seeing is not based on our sense of wonder, then we only suppose we see but do not do so in fact. The same goes for hearing and all of our other senses.

Our sense of wonder must be trained. We are born with it but all too soon we lose it. This is because we are not schooled or trained in it but instead we are schooled and trained in the perception of sense data, which is not really perception but an enactment of aversion to the light. Sense data appeal to our ego and can be classified, so that we experience a sense of control over our environment, to the exclusion of any actual contact with it.

Sense data also exert a temptation on our perceptive soul. The reason for this is so that we may learn to be careful with what we believe. When we allow ourselves, carelessly, to be duped by sense data, often for no other reason than that they are around, we begin to believe what goes contrary to our sense of wonder. Our ego wishes to believe whatever exists, however true existence cannot really be appreciated by us when we are egotistic, so we end up believing a lot of nonsense, which we then endeavour to make public so that others will believe it too. Finally, as things go, there is not all that much that is worth believing. Those who equate having faith with believing run aground here if some ego-stimulus, due to presented sense data, comes their way but they do not disallow it.

Any degree of enlightenment causes us to become suspicious of sense data, in other words of information that appeals merely to our senses or to our reason, to the exclusion of our sense of wonder. As we become more practiced in this sense of wonder we also become more impermeable to sense data and less tempted.

*

The organ of our sense of wonder is our childish or reformed heart. Just as a child, before the has been spoilt, sees around him the real world and senses reality, so does any human being whose heart has become attached to an unreal world and then was reformed.

Nothing is more important to a lapsed human being than the reformation of his heart. If we were to name all the differences between the lapsed and the reformed human heart we would never come to an end. And yet there are certain common initial experiences that bring it home to someone that not all is well with him in this department. I will mention only a few here. There is the experience of such loneliness, especially in a crowd, that the whole world seems swamped with indifference and aggression. There is the overpowering *boredom* with everything that causes so many to commit suicide. There is the deep *disappointment* after a loss, the *despair* over hope gone passive or dead. Also there is the *anger* over not being able to achieve our goal after such a long time of striving. Or what about the realization that we cannot after all help ourselves but need the help of someone else?

Common to all these is a more or less painful insight. Rarely can this insight be articulated right from the beginning. However some consciousness of our being able to express ourselves always exists. Even if it amounts to nothing more than a wail of outrage, a cry of terror or a fit of weeping, the consoling possibility of an extreme utterance may be taken for a sign that a way out exists for us. It is a way out of our heartless condition.

We have to be careful here, because heartlessness does not mean the same to everyone. He who does not weep at his mother's funeral is not necessarily heartless. Nor is everyone who weeps necessarily in the possession of a valuable insight into his heartlessness. What we wish to emphasize here are the consequences of a life led under conditions of falsehood. When a way out becomes possible for us we may be shocked to the core. Sometimes a mere glimpse of the terrible fact is enough to incapacitate us for an appreciable time. It is time for us to go into ourselves to aid and abet the healing process which will allow us eventually to enjoy real world.

Needless to say, while we pursue the path of inward reparation, we recall that the world we have hitherto taken for granted is certainly not real. We turn away from it, not because something is wrong with it but because we are no longer able to appreciate it. We lack the organ to do so because we have been misled and because we have

4

allowed ourselves to be misled. No use pretending that the blame is not ours at all. However, all blame to one side, what is essential for us to do is to turn inward in the knowledge that we are wrong. We are in the wrong and we would like to find the right way.

This simple combination of insight and intention in terms of a change of heart is what is meant by repentance. A sentimental shift in the direction of a sorrowful change of belief is something else altogether.

Or let us rather leave this business of repentance to one side for the time being because it is so intensely charged with attitudes within the Christian religion. For our own purpose here let us simply keep in mind that reformation of heart means a coming to terms with that inner urgency of the light, so no wonder that the world as we have come to mistake it has to be left to one side for the time being. Why should we bother passing judgment on it? I wonder, for example, why so much religion in the East rejects the outside world as a mere veil of deception. Why is there so little promise, if any, of that world that is eventually returned to us in its magnificence and splendour once our crucial sense of wonder is re-established? Not the created world is deceiving, or deceptive but our fundamental organ of perception has become faulty. We look at beings and see nothing but things.

So we turn inward and what we come up against is perhaps quite horrendous. We experience doubt, insecurity, discomfort and the like. Most of all what we experience is the fear of being negated, of being discounted and wiped out. We notice that our heart is no longer the organ of that sense of wonder that would allow us to appreciate worldly beauty and truth but we might almost say that it has become possessed by a variety of demons that threaten our expulsion from the realm within. Quickly we close our eyes because we certainly do not want this to be true. All the same, the light urges us to persevere with our reconnaissance of our inward condition and state. For some time we may hasten back and forth between response to the urgency of the light and flight from what such responses reveal to us.

*

Once we have decided to work at analyzing the chaos within us, we do well to search, perhaps by trial and error, for a method, so that we proceed in a productive direction and don't end up moving in disconcerting circles.

It is very likely that once we have dedicated ourselves to the task in hand, deciding once and for all not to return to the world picture, the false world picture that we have negligently allowed to appear, the tumult within will for the time being be still. While we still blame our circumstances and hold others responsible for our distorted or totally lacking sense of world appreciation, the tumult continues. However a totally forgiving disposition takes care of that.

The momentary calm within is no solution. Regard it rather as an opportunity for choosing your tools, your weapons, for planning your first approach to the darkness within in the name of enlightenment. It does however occur as a result of your intentional and earnest application. Whatever is to happen next depends on your next move.

If you can recall that what has urged you to set out on this path was the light, you may well decide to proceed in the name of this light. You would then be light-conscious. You would, in other words, hold firmly in your mind – you would mean – that you have arrived here, face to face with the insistent uproar, in response to the urgent light within.

If you were to do this, something rather crucial would take place. Let us call it the segregation of good spirits. Your light-consciousness is productive in this particular way, in that it informs you of a difference between good and bad in your heart. Your initial move, your determined approach to the pandemonium in yourself, with the questionable or ambiguous world picture put to one side, resulted in – was productive of – a stillness, a hush within, as if the various agents of confusion were waiting for your next move. This next move, your light-consciousness – i.e. your recalling that you have after all set out in this inward direction not because you had nothing more pleasant to do but in response to an experienced urgency which you have learned to call the light – is productive in that it allows you to distinguish good spirits, to discern between good and bad agents of turmoil.

Why is it helpful that you separate these good spirits? These beneficial daemons? Well, that should be self-explanatory. Picture it like this: they have been struggling with the bad demons for possession of your heart. Let's call it a struggle of the daemons versus the demons. Now you come along, in the name of the light, and you say to those daemons: 'Here, to me!' As far as they are concerned you stand engulfed in light. Could anything be more welcome to them?

*

So here now you have the first part of your method. You may call it the segregation of the daemons. These are tutelary spirits with no will of their own. You are ready now, in their company, for your first piece of human natural work. What shall it be? These tutelary spirits have only this on task, which is to inform you, over the succeeding days, weeks, months and years, to bless you with particular elements of wisdom which you will transform into communicable thought – to be materialised in the light of day and as light of day.

These will be your works. At first you will work rather strenuously under the compulsion of the light. All your senses are solely metaphysical. You do not bother with world or with anything to do with world. All you have known of the world so far has at last been unmasked as insufficiently perceived and you have turned to your organs of perception, I dare say in order to repair them. If ever they are to be capable of a physical perception of what is real, they must learn to operate in the universally present light. This implies your personal cooperation with the light, as it urges you to inward action and then sustains you in your work of shedding light of day in the light of day.

I have described the inward action as a segregation of daemons, of good, tutelary spirits, in your heart. What goes on with the bad tutelary spirits, the demons, meanwhile? They too long to enter the light of day. They have no will, only this longing. Their tuition, however, is of no practical use. By that I mean that they cannot add to the light of day, in which all human beings seek to disport themselves.

What these useless spirits, these demons, would teach you is that the present metaphysical reality is the be-all and end-all of human survival and life. In other words they will not condescend to be put to work as creative principles of the light of day.

It is certainly possible to take up with these bad spirits and to participate in astonishing spiritual marvels. Amazing transformations of elemental nature become possible and are acted out by the illuminate for the benefit of those who would join them in their metaphysical endgame. How enticing, how tempting are these enactments of a spectral light that first borrows, then requisitions your will, so that it may ensconce itself in what I would call 'the dark of day'!

The major difference, then, between the good tuition and the bad tuition, between the daemons and the demons, is that the former, with the help of your willingness and your willing immersion in their longing, make it possible for you to create works that stand revealed in the light of day and amount to a blessed shedding of this light of day, so that we may worship with restored senses in reality and in full appreciation of the world-feast, as I would like to call it – while the latter, if we allow ourselves to be consoled by them, will fetter us permanently, self-consciously, in a dead-end spirituality. Not that these demons will neglect to preach humility and love, however it will be love in the interest of separation from 'this world', from the world as a veil of mere appearance and not love for the sake of world as concrete reality.

*

We should not think that these demons are evil. They are just bad. Those who go along with them are bad. Evil is something else. It is the drastic down-side of good. It opposes good, both actively and passively. Once you have begun to pay heed to the urge that causes you to confront the turmoil in your heart you have moved beyond evil. What you come across in your heart is good and bad, not good and evil. If you take no notice of your heart, then its contents are evil and in your ignorance you let evil come into the world. Thousands today are overjoyed when they face up to the chaos inside themselves because now they are beyond evil. A little gladness would be appropriate alright but joy, this supreme joy they manifest, is, I'm afraid, premature. If they take up with what is bad now they sell themselves short. What is bad is useless alright, compared to the good, but it is worse than useless because it habituates us to the non-good, to the not yet good. They speak ever so often of their spiritual intoxication, these imbibers of the bad, of the not-good and that is the sign of habituation to the bad. They speak of love, of joy, of humility, and that is certainly to be preferred to the evil they would otherwise do, however it is the spirit of an impersonal, or even of 'the' impersonal god, they worship. They do not worship in reality but in a trance. It's amazing what they get up to. However the peak of their daily existence is *individual innocence* and not *personal excellence*.

*

In order to discover the light within us and to become capable of personal excellence, we have to do more than just disemburden ourselves of our ego. Certainly this is essential if ever we hope to express ourselves. However if our aim goes beyond that and if we cannot find satisfaction in any creed, then we must cooperate with those daemons and, through them, with the light they present. We must have a will not merely to individual innocence but to personal excellence. It depends, as you see, on the nature of our will, whether we and those who know our works benefit from the light or else at best from illusion, which does not work.

So we shouldn't imagine that we might have demons and segregated daemons in front of us in a sense where we might then decide in some way for one of the other according to detectable attributes. No, it is simply our will, our informed will, that decides the matter for us. You might almost say that we choose according to who we are – except that a personal willingness is surely up to us. Here is where the word fits: 'The true shepherd knows his sheep and they recognize his voice and follow him.' For the purpose of this dissertation we may profitably think of the daemons as the sheep known by the true shepherd.

So the disorder of our emotions and feelings, as soon as we begin to object to it, may be approached in this fashion. Our awareness of the disorder quietens things down, so that we may then intend to work up the good emotions and feelings while ignoring the rest. It is work and nothing less than work, that we mean the light and mind it in person. You see how possible it would be here too to interpret this experience of disorderly emotion entirely negatively and merely to want to be rid of the experience of it. Surely a chemical drug would accomplish as much. But then it is more honourable to face the enemy. So even if we do not know that this emotional turmoil is due to an urgency of the divine light, we might be able to effect a bit of harmony simply by assuming some half decently objective stance. Unless we acknowledge the creative, work-oriented light however, we will get no further than a momentary respite followed by perhaps even worse disorder. If, on the other hand, we persevere, what counts is whether we do so as individuals or as persons.

Since so much depends on whether we do the one or the other, it might be just as well to say a few words in explication of individuality and personality. The latter implies the sort of ethical responsibility, which in its finest and noblest form, takes all of life and all that lives into consideration. It matters to you as a person how I as a human being am, because you value community, or any kind of personal interaction. As an individual, by comparison, you care mainly for yourself. You have an eye out for your advantage, readily at the expense of others.

Also, on a more wide-ranging plane, the great illusionists in the present and past have always taken pride in being able to surmount the constraints of space and time, while as persons, on the contrary, we value these so-called constraints and are grateful for them even if only for simplicity's sake. Individuals reject personality because it threatens their belief in infinite liberty. Persons take pity on individuals because they would like them to enjoy freedom. The understanding of the difference between liberty which allows for possibilities, and freedom, which is bedded in reality, is not of negligible importance here. Also, let's not forget that space and time are, after all, misunderstood right from the beginning along with the world and as the basic aspects of the world, so that the overcoming of the world, which is an individual's only approach to reality, also implies a negation of space and time. Once again, one would wonder why the overcoming of a supposed enemy does not lead on to a befriending of him.

It stands to reason that not until some degree of liberty has been gained can it become evident that the world was mis-perceived in the beginning. It is that anyone should settle down in this individual liberty rather than moving on to personal freedom that strikes us as so deplorable. Naturally those who have no intention of passing on to a positive world view will mistake their liberty for freedom.

We can surely see how personality is itself a work of world affirmation, when we begin to see and know the world as world, in its true light. He who would know the world in that same true light that initially urged him to 'clear his eye' must take upon him the responsibility of personhood. This means ignoring all those individual liberties and rights on which he has been insisting and depending and learning how to love and care for others. Even the light then reveals itself in person. The world, that mythic being, stands revealed now simply as world, in light, more specifically in the light of day.

World is emphatically young for those who are young and mature for the mature. Drastic measures have been taken by the old to renew the world, but according to our present understanding that must be pointless.

*

Once again: The contents of the human heart are evil until we become aware of them. Evil is brought into the world by those who exist in their egocentric security and behave self-righteously. They have neither idea nor thought that they do this. The light does not urge them but they are driven by bad intellect and ill will. Those who seek out their company, for whatever reason, soon join them.

When the light urges us we first of all feel constrained to depart from those who are egocentric and self-righteous. We feel inclined to come out from among them, usually on account of the burden they unconsciously lay on us.

Next we discover in ourselves, or in our hearts, a commotion of motivations, a chaos of emotions, feelings and passions; opinions, thoughts and ideas; good, bad and indifferent. Upon reflection, meditation and contemplation we are able to segregate the good from the bad and indifferent. If we take up with the good, our eventual reward will be bliss. Taking up with the bad, the best we can hope for is ecstasy.

The difference between bliss and ecstasy is crucial. It is bliss to experience the presence of the light. When we do, we understand that ecstasy is no longer a viable condition of our heart.

*

Bliss is human-natural happiness. It is not happiness because of anything gained or accomplished. We cannot attain to bliss, not by repeating mantras nor by works, however self-sacrificial or other-oriented.

Bliss is human nature perfectly realized. It is not a state attendant upon perfectly realized human nature but that nature itself. Once experienced, it cannot be destroyed. We may stray from it but are always able to return to it.

Our human nature is known to us from the beginning. Infants are not in any doubt about their human nature. Nonetheless the notion of bliss would puzzle them. Little by little awareness intercedes. Due to it, our nature becomes real.

Realized human nature is blissful. Imagine the absence of all psychic phenomena. Purity of soul is taken for granted. Gone are all pretences of self. Instead imagine environmental experience. Thought and sensation are one. This means that neither mind nor body is separately identifiable. Experience therefore is perfectly physical.

Now let's compare ecstasy to bliss. It may be attained through trance. It is a state when the mind is overly excited or the body overly stimulated. To be in a trance means to invite disorderly experience, when either the mind is removed from the body or the body is abstracted from the mind.

Whatever is initiated in such a state cannot bear fruit. An ecstatic trance limits the function of our sense organs and tempts us to participate in spiritual aberrations. These are then compared to materialistic states of body and mind and because they are extraordinary they are valued.

The ecstatic trance depends on bad spirits. Spiritual experience is not necessarily worth anything. Good spirit makes it possible for us to have life and to live. Bad spirits offer intoxication and endless, pointless survival. Good spirit is remarkable in that it draws to our attention our shortcomings while at the same time offering fulfilment. Bad spirits offer a bogus fulfilment for which no identification of shortcomings is required.

*

Anything that furthers the parting of mind from body or body from mind rather than joining the two is surely pernicious. This is not to say that there are not many false combinations of the two that would need to be undone before the true reality of the two as one might be effected. However, as I intimated above, those who would have us stop at the distinction or even separation of the two and then see either mind or body perform prodigious miracles, do themselves and us a disservice. The mind on its own can cause us to levitate, to peruse the future and read present happenings in distant lands. Are we to take these aberrations for advantages? Indeed let us not. Feet on solid ground and a respectful appreciation of the here and now – these are rare enough blessings and we do well to work towards deserving them. This means, among other things, steering clear of these intentional miracles and spirit-intoxications that are sometimes appraised as worthy acquirements in some Eastern popular cultures where the particular resistance of matter is just plain not valued. Against that we have in the West, until just recently, thought so highly of matter that desire for possession and control of it has had us innumerable times at one another's throats. It is a fatuous judgment that would seek mutual advantage for both halves of the earth by throwing the decayed fruits of spiritualism into a common pot with the premature fruits of materialism.

To make a still finer point of it: Energy in matter is a fact. It has not always been a fact. Ignorance of this fact is forgivable but those who insist on playing fast and loose with energy and matter as distinct and readily interchangeable items should perhaps not be cheated of the consequences. But that is an uncharitable thought. Nonetheless, the best we can hope for is that lessons will be learned before it is too late.

It is indeed a great pleasure to be able to rely on gravity, yes, even to the point when it sharpens our wits when we tumble into a hole for the lack of them. And as for the here and now, well, while it may be true that only those who have experienced it know how to praise it, there is nevertheless much that can be usefully done by those who desire to profit from their example.

It is in the here and now that we thrive as human beings; that we grow and mature and bear fruit.

*

Body separate from mind means materialism. Mind separate from body means spiritualism.

The materialist vaunts his borrowed strength. This strength attaches to things. In other words, strength, for him, resides in the things he desires and acquires.

Although a materialist views matter as an extension of his body, he cannot properly appreciate it because due to his mentality he is bound to keep it at a distance. There he manipulates it, invents laws for it and persuades himself that he is in touch with something real. In fact what he does removes him from reality. He experiences a periodicity of fortune, (not good or bad, just fortune). He learns to ride these periods out until he is too tired to care whether, by his lights, he succeeds or fails. The things he has produced naturally wear out and fall apart, including his world picture.

The light is nothing for the materialist except something to hide from. From his point off view, he avoids metaphysics. The golden rule for him is that reality must be quantifiable. His approach to language is that of the traditionalist and the specialist. He would be ready to cry on the shoulder of Dame Nature if he could make her out in the mist of his mercurial refinements. Alas, she teases him with forces and laws, with disguised principles and pretexts for good moods.

In the presence of a materialist we notice how our human nature shrinks into itself. We feel we ought to come up with ameliorative judgments but at the same time we feel stymied, so up against an indistinct imagination. The best we can do is be still and project some hopeful good will. This has caused many a materialist to pause in his tracks.

*

The spiritualist is ever on the look-out for tomorrow. He lives, or rather exists, as if tomorrow were today. If he makes any announcements, they always impinge on 'common ground'. By common ground I mean that basis on which all human beings, of whatever race or skin colour, relate and communicate. For the spiritualist such common ground is of no interest because, from his point of view, you cannot land on it and take off again. His rationality is promiscuous. The very suggestion of taking root, of solidarity with physical reality or of consanguinity with life is repulsive to him, however in a way which he gladly mistakes for moral judgment. Like all of us, unless he is to emerge from his error he must condemn his fault in others and in the world around him.

*

Matter is particles of resistance. Spirit is what moves and motivates all creatures. This we understand and it makes proper sense to us as soon as our own body and mind are physically one. At that stage we are enlightened, by the light that is universally present. We are also able properly to know all that exists. What we know then, from our enlightened point of view, reveals itself to us as it truly is and not in some guise or as it were behind a veil or "through a glass darkly". We are also able to tell whether something exists or not. We will be in no doubt as to the distinction between beings and ephemera or phantoms. This is because, metaphorically speaking, our feet are on common ground. Here we welcome all that makes sense to us, in the accompanying knowledge that if it makes sense to us it is real. You might say that we have an extra sense, according to which we may be certain.

If we now know matter as particular resistance, such as when we stand on a floor or pickup an apple, we are in no way experiencing it as removed from physical reality and separate from spirit. The point here is that enlightened experience of physical reality comes to us and is available to us in every being of which we are certain. Remember that we are certain of what makes sense to us and that whatever makes sense to us does so not because it confirms our suspicion about something or is in agreement with an opinion we have held for some time but solely because our mind and body are one. We distinguish therefore between spurious certainty and real certainty, the latter being an aspect of an enlightened human being's experience.

If we are motivated to stand on a floor or to pick up an apple, spirit is the cause or origin of that. This we may know without further ado. However before we may be certain that we are motivated by good spirit and not by bad or indifferent spirit we may have to initiate good will in ourselves and then, to the extent that we continue to be motivated to stand on that floor or to pick up that apple, we may be certain of good spirit as our motivation.

We can never have a reasonable wish to identify bad or indifferent spirit. All that matters to us is that the spirit that moves or motivates us is good and to that end we initiate good will. This is no problem for an enlightened human being because he is aware of good spirit within himself. He may know this doctrinally or from personal experience. Good will, in his case, is therefore nothing more than his personal assent to the manifestation of that spirit. If his initiation of good will results in him being less or no longer motivated, then he knows where he stands.

*

20

For the enlightened human being, good will is his ticket to blissful living. Once he knows that his good will facilitates manifestations of good spirit on common ground, he quickly sets about making a habit of it. On numerous occasions he will correct his action or the line of his aspiration by subjecting it to what he knows of the light, which is good spirit, within him. You look out the window and in the distance you see the dark silhouette of a church steeple against cloud behind it. Very gradually the two move in opposite directions. You correct what seems to be the case by knowing that the steeple only appears to move. You refer to the knowledge you have of the steeple as stationary, so the clouds alone must be moving. You look again, and there the steeple moves again, so that once more you may correct your perception of reality. In the same way you know that good spirit within you moves and motivates you to behaviour and action that you decide upon with increasingly effective reference to good spirit within you.

Gradually an enlightened human being's good will becomes all-pervasive, so that he perceives with good will too. Incidentally, there are no degrees of good will. There is no better will, only good will. Good spirit within us is simple and clear and we either behave in solidarity with it or not. Human beings are, however, more or less enlightened and this refers to the amount or degree of motivation they can sustain at any given time. They will be able to come up with good will, but greater works rely on more good will.

Meanwhile I dare say we may have to be reminded that good spirit within us is not only good but also powerful. It is not 'only' good but 'powerful' good. We can see now even more clearly why we cannot sustain good spirit within us until our mind and body are one and we are physically sound. Any detailed description of how we may achieve such physical soundness or solidity goes beyond our intentions for the present essay.

An enlightened human being, whose body and mind are one and who can therefore be certain of physical experience also because he is able to initiate good will in himself, must ask himself how he imagines himself to be a creature of flesh. There is this visible aspect of himself and he is bound to feel the need to account for it. He may not feel content with calling it the mystery of creation, especially if time and again he experiences pain.

Body and mind as one in themselves – in itself – cannot account for pain. Neither can it account for the visible aspect of things – and I say 'things' advisedly, because I do not mean beings. On the other hand we have all undergone a degree of indoctrination in terms of such a concept as incarnation, where we imagine something called spirit suddenly becoming flesh. Or we entertain an opinion, more or less organized publicly, of spirit of some description having somehow become flesh in the past so that now, spontaneously, we have this – whatever we wish to call it, at our disposal. If what we habitually call history, or the past, intervenes between us and it, we are advised to believe that it does not. Keep in mind how ready we are to picture – I say 'picture' advisedly, not meaning 'imagine' – the past and all the things that pertain to it.

If we are to make certain sense of incarnate spirit as historically initiated and generated we will have to come up with good will even in the face of pain. This can be explained in the following way. Pain, we must know, to the extent and degree of it, informs us of our readiness for incarnate spirit. By intelligently suffering pain, an enlightened human being takes incarnate spirit upon himself. All that interferes with – or would diminish – his blissful existence, informs him in this way of his readiness for available incarnate spirit. He appropriates what is available to him in this way by means of informed and intelligent suffering. Soon he learns, through direct individual experience, that incarnate spirit is indeed real.

The purpose of intelligent suffering, and of the efficacy of it, is so that we may be certain of incarnate spirit as real. A hedonistic society makes no allowance for such spirit. Therefore pain remains at best a mysterious threat against which one has to defend oneself. Also it is not known as such but as an infinite variety of pains, each one of which seems to require a defence peculiar to it. Also, since hedonism does not allow for the oneness of body and mind, it has to try to cope with pains of the body and pains of the mind, and so on, while so-called psychosomatic pains do not testify inadvertently, as it might seem, to a oneness of body and mind but rather directly to their separateness.

Once an enlightened human being has sufficiently informed himself – or been informed through practice – of the efficacy of the intelligent suffering of pain for appropriation of incarnate spirit, he will find himself being urged to progress from the individual to the personal dimension of incarnate spirit. He no longer needs pain to remind and inform him of what he knows now with certainty, having learned it through teaching and practice. It is the pain of others that interests him now. Through individual practice he has acquired the tools for personal suffering and it is the difference between individual and personal suffering that will now become clear to him.

Eventually now the enlightened human being will be able to think and feel incarnate spirit. Those in his mental or physical proximity who are in pain he loves. What this does for him and for them is quite an eye-opener for him at first. Let's call to mind that he is passing from a principally passive to a primarily active mode of behaviour. Suffering, even intelligent suffering, when he knows what he is about, is passive. Once he begins to love, personally, he is primarily active and secondarily passive. He is now personally active whereas previously he was individually passive.

Now that he actively makes room in himself for the pain of others, he becomes aware, communally, of *the* incarnate spirit. He gets to know it as flesh and spirit as one, in person.

Further, he does not have to wait until those in his proximity are in pain before he personally loves them. As long as he does so when they are in pain – and it would seem safe to assume that all are in some manner, inwardly or outwardly in pain – he will not become indifferent to those who are unaware of any pain.

(By the way, reading is something most of us do quite a lot and it might pay us to consider that this same attitude of intelligent suffering or passivity to the imagined writer, or indeed our active love of him while we read since he is after all in our mental presence, will most readily reveal to us what, of his matter, makes sense to us

24

and what does not. Or let's put it this way: We are certain to benefit more from the work of a writer if we approach his work and him with good will than with criticism, for example, or merely with curiosity. A critique, of course, is something else.)

*

We can both think and feel incarnate spirit in person. Are we creatures of flesh when we know (think and feel) incarnate spirit? Can we personally know incarnate spirit and be in pain? What I am getting at is that we should not suppose we are always creatures of flesh just because now and again we are in pain. Of course there are ways of making sure that we are always in pain and that is by organizing ourselves. The great organizers of mankind are those who are most afraid of incarnate spirit. They know that by fitting us into categories and keeping us there we will not be at risk of discovering that incarnate spirit exists, and that our flesh, once it is really ours, can quite readily be handed over to that spirit, whereupon we will no longer need anyone to watch over us.

It stands to reason that the great organizers will not admit they are afraid of incarnate spirit. Nonetheless they do act out of fear. You might also say they are creatures of flesh and unwilling to be otherwise. They know about the possibility of incarnate spirit but they will not entertain anyone's realization of it – neither their own nor anyone else's.

It behoves us therefore to ask ourselves to what extent do we organize human beings and other beings. Are we afraid of what will happen if we relinquish this need to organize? Do we suppose that organization will afford us greater and speedier success? Is what we can lay a finger on or point out to one another more real because of that?

*

We have to take a look now at this organization which makes the thinking and feeling of incarnate spirit impossible because it puts in its place the thought and feeling of general or particular togetherness in the name of some abstract conception. As soon as some such abstract conception is in place, it has to be so in our mind as separate from our body. More accurately, since mind separate from body cannot really be ours, such an abstract concept prevents us from owning our mind and body as one. However, as we have shown, our mind and body as one is what we work for so that we may indeed think and feel incarnate spirit in person. Therefore any such organizational spirit counteracts our initiative and fetters us to a conception of ourselves as aggregate members of a circumscribed mass.

Of course it is always important for us to lead an orderly existence. Order and organization are sometimes confused, such as when we rebel against being organized by becoming disorderly. Also we are much more likely to have abstract organization foisted upon us if we allow our existence to become disorderly. Furthermore, if we order our existence in terms of incarnate spirit, then any attempt by any organization to make us bow to and abide by its demands is mysteriously frustrated. I say mysteriously because ordinary reason cannot explain this. Inexplicable exceptions are made, fortunate accidents happen, general interventions by blind forces work in our favour. Time and again we cannot but marvel at the seemingly charmed life we lead. We may take this in stride, of course, and there is no reason whatsoever for explanation or interpretation, as long as we keep in mind that it is our part to lead an orderly existence in the name of incarnate spirit in person.

An orderly existence in terms of incarnate spirit and in the name of the incarnate spirit in person obviously cannot spring from carnal or spiritualist concerns for survival advantages. (Spiritualist survival we touched on when we mentioned such states as trance and ecstasy.) We no longer calculate or plan exclusively in terms of the flesh or the spirit once we are protectively overshadowed by that spirit in which and in whom the very power of god is actively operative. Merciful good spirit, which is god's providential or paternal aspect, is eternally powerful within the incarnate spirit of our temporal communication.

*

We can hand our flesh over to the incarnate spirit. This is a spiritual act of love for the particular aim and purpose of our perfection. As we hand our flesh over we are perfected.

I am describing a process here which takes as long as it takes. It cannot be understood except in conjunction with every element of 'persecution' we experience.

Persecution? Incarnate spirit is never out of danger. Put as simply as possible: If we want the advantages of it, we have to be willing to fight for it.

Who, or what, is the enemy of incarnate spirit? Materialism and spiritualism. Is there any chance of these enemies ever overcoming the incarnate spirit? None whatsoever. This spirit is not, after all, itself in danger or at risk. It is we who are in danger, we in our solidarity with it, we in our championing of its aim, which is our perfection, our wholeness as human beings.

What we require in order to be perfected is organic consolidarity with the incarnate spirit in person. What this organic consolidarity amounts to is an overcoming, in ourselves, of every effect or affect of materialism or spiritualism, but with the help of incarnate spirit.

Shall we say that incarnate spirit needs us to overcome its enemies? That would be nonsense. We need the aid of incarnate spirit to overcome the enemies of our consolidarity with it. That is the truth and the sense of it.

The term 'organic' points to the fact that every one of our organs may be involved in what is after all work, and more specifically loving work. Since enemies are at the gate, love is of the essence, so that every effect or affect of those two persecuting enemies may be creatively faced.

*

Genuine art facilitates our work in this department. The achievement, time and again, of consolidarity with incarnate spirit is the most important work any human being can do.

Time and again individuals surface in various culture-realms who find it impossible to do survival work. They recognize within themselves the need to work for something other than their continual existence on the surface of the earth. They need to be told that they may well be among those whose task it is to learn all that is necessary for them eventually to introduce incarnate spirit into the growing community of men, women and children, who live in the light of day. Those of us who know of this need will never tire of helping such individuals to identify themselves correctly, so that they may gain confidence in their extraordinary way of life. Their eventual contribution to human communality will be historically unique and new, so they need all the support they can get from us while they work out their incomparable personality. Many organizations will try to get them under their control so as to align them materialistically or spiritualistically. What we can do meanwhile, if we suppose we have indentified them correctly, is to keep them in mind of their special status, which is not a matter of vanity but of a profound ethical responsibility, which cuts across traditional moral dogma and conventional social strictures. They themselves must eventually decide whether they have what it takes to add their original voice to the chorus of voices that upholds the hegemony of truth in reality.

*

If we are to assume that it is the effects and affects of materialism and spiritualism that 'persecute' us, when otherwise we might be perfectly at ease, then should we not try to pre-empt such effects, to get ahead of them and to 'draw their sting', so to speak, before they can get at us?

Alas, we are not here to be at ease. At least that is not to be our central ambition in life. When we suppose that it might be, we inadvertently fall into one of the major affects of spiritualism, which is idealism. It teaches us, or at least would persuade us, that with a bit of effort now we will finally be at ease. We allow an ideal to be implanted in our brain by some organization such as the

State (fight the war to end all wars!) and if we manage to come out on the other side we blame that organization for letting us down. How many people have not been 'betrayed' by Communism, by Capitalism, by Hedonism or Buddhism, simply because they allowed such an ideal to be implanted in their brains, whereupon all sane and sensible pursuits came to an end!

A materialistic effect that can plague us for a long time – indeed it lengthens time out of all decent proportions – is the notion of 'the fix'. The thinking here is that if only we get our thinking and behaviour right, all that is of value must follow – indeed cannot help but follow. If it does not, then the machine we operate is broken and must be fixed.

From the materialistic point of view we are machines, which need to be understood, maintained and, if broken, fixed.

From the spiritualistic point of view we are mere expressions of spirit and so we need to find the spirit that will express us in the most flattering fashion.

In truth, however, human beings are neither machines nor spirits but – human beings. It's quite impossible, as a matter of fact, to say that human beings are anything else. Animals are like human beings but that does not turn human beings into animals. What we have to come to grips with is the special status of human beings but that means that first of all we have to look past the machine and the spirit in ourselves and seek the human being. This can be a lifelong preoccupation, even after we have learned to identify materialistic and spiritualistic organizations and their affects and effects.

I keep mentioning affects and effects because given our being whole in mind and body as one, the 'persecution' is in essence such that we are either affected bodily, separating body, or effected mentally, separating mind. The persecution is of our mind as separate or of our body as separate. In other words, two things happen. A duality of mind and body comes about in the sense that our whole being, our whole human being, is disrupted and either the body as separate, affectively, or the mind as separate, effectively, is put under stress and consequently in pain.

We need to understand this correctly, otherwise we will try to fix the separate body or heal the separate mind, unaware of the deeper need for mind and body to be one and physically whole.

*

Whole human beings are not fictions or ideals – or myths, for that matter. We cannot have any reasonable notion at all of the role played by materialism and spiritualism if we do not begin with our knowledge of whole human beings, who can properly and with right speak of 'their' bodies and 'their' minds. When they do so, they know that they do not refer to separate entities but, so to speak, to the face and obverse aspect of their soul. If they only had to concern themselves with other human beings, who are whole in themselves, they would come right out with it and speak of their soul and themselves as one and the same. It would mean the same to them whether they said: My soul praises god, or: I praise god. It would not be a sensible question for them if you asked them: Alright, your soul may be immortal but what about you?

Whole, or healed, human beings are not monads that float freely in some imaginary or abstract space but they suffer persecution and they work. The persecution is like a following but for wrong reasons or from bad motives. Human beings are not only directive but also attractive (see my 'Creative Philosophy'). It is the attractiveness that accounts for the wrong and bad following; for the persecution. We set personal examples and these are perceived, misunderstood or envied. We choose to live among those who are wicked throughout, so that is what we expect. We learn how to deal with it. That is our work.

Technically, our work is not limited to responses to persecution, but those account for our works, which are influential in time and space. We work and we produce works. The latter would not actually be possible unless there were a sufficiency of the former.

Of course there are many ways of thinking about this and one way might be that we keep out a weather eye for any symptomatic separation of our body or mind, as they turn into 'a' body or 'a' mind. There was probably a time when we were ignorant enough to suppose that there could never be such a thing as thought or feeling that was not our own. We did not realize how we were almost constantly affected or effected in such a way that our thoughts and feelings happened to us and we were subjected or even enslaved by them, as we may observe plainly in extreme cases such as obsession or rage, not to mention morbid longings, and nursed grievances. Meanwhile we have learned that the two can be made one again, as they were at birth and that our reappropriation of our mind and body, the healing of our soul, in other words, and therefore of ourselves, is something to be sought, to be worked for and even something to be demonstrated in our works. It should be evident, for example, in what I write here, that the meaning of it cannot be materialistically grasped or spiritualistically followed. Nearly every sentence contains a stumbling block for those who would attempt it. I am quite ready to be ignored or scolded. If I am, I would hope to be able to accept cheerfully such confirmation of my knowledge and understanding.

*

When the light exists as world (not as *the* world), we have said, we call it light. World is not mythic. Light influences us in our search for positive world experience. None of our senses can cope with light unless it is represented by beings. World experience is sensible acquaintance with beings. We should never suppose we can experience world in the absence of light.

So for example we may see (or sense) a being in front of us and engage with it knowledgeably. We too are beings but we are specifically human beings and this allows us to approach other beings knowledgeably. As we know the being in front of us, we step into relation with it and this relation is of benefit both to it and to us. Let us assume that this being in front of us and in a relation with us is not a human being but perhaps an artificial being, such as what someone has manufactured or made. How can our knowledgeable approach to it be of benefit not only to us but to it too?

The benefit we mean here is *world propriety* and a greater degree of it. What we know participates to that degree not only in its own being but in world being. It is no use pretending that anything is known other than what I know and you are bound to say the same. The knowledge we mean here is not derived from sense data but rests on the basis of a sense of wonder. Not until we communicate can there be something like shared knowledge, or community.

World propriety is due to light and to our participation in it. World is not known to those who rely on sense data and who draw their information from such data. By *world propriety* I mean how beings are held in mutual world relationship. When we speak of 'our world', or when I speak of 'my world' and you of yours, what we refer to is the sum total of all beings that stand in fitting relation both to one another and to us. How many such beings make up your world? Perhaps not many at all. How many days have passed since you have gained such intimate knowledge of yet one more being?

The infinity of world will not in truth occur to us until we have shared our world in communal knowledge and understanding. Individual world is closed and finite. Personal world is infinite. When I speak to you I soon find out whether you have taken that crucial step from the individual and social to the personal and communal.

From the point of view of our individuality we are quite right to assume that nothing really exists except what we know to exist. Why should we take anyone else's word for something we have to experience before we can be sure?

An individual, which means a human being who insists on the rightness of his world to the point where his mind is so closed and his body so anaesthetized that he will not take that step to personal communication and community, will sooner or later succumb to morbidity and nothing anyone can do or say will persuade him to contemplate the possibility of infinite world. He mistakes his finite world for the source of all knowledge, real and possible.

The role played by light every time we transcend individualism (insistence on our individuality) can be clearly understood. The signs of light-influence and the symptoms of our reluctance to see it are melancholy, a morose temperament, a sense of being at the end of our tether and the apparent or felt need to break out of an assumed oppression. Since we are born with a natural proclivity for communal existence in world community, we have cause to be grateful for these signs that make it difficult for us to be content as individuals in society. In other words, light spurs us on towards maturity in world community.

*

The main question we need to ask ourselves therefore is how to see this light and how to remain aware of it. It is the light that also shines in the darkness, so that we can see even the darkness. However as soon as we search it out, this light, it disappears from view and leaves us with what we can know and understand. So we may say that thanks to light (not the light) we see beings again and not just things.

So what are the characteristic of beings, that we may distinguish them from things?

It is we ourselves, due to our enlightened knowledge and understanding, that see beings and not things. Certainly no one in his right mind wants to see things. They are the products of our mistaken knowledge and faulty understanding.

Why should light be an ordinant of our awareness? So that we may be judiciously aware. This means that not only what attracts our attention is seen by us but also what is worth seeing and does not attract our attention.

If light were always in our mind, (even at night) we would never fall short of the joys of universal creation. So what can we do so that this light never leaves us in the lurch? We can ask for it always to inform us, whatever we do and wherever we go.

We can turn this into a universally creative request. We may have experienced this light off and on, and how determined we are that we should never lose sight of if again! Alas, there comes a time again when we are surrounded by things and cannot see clearly.

If light is to inform us reliably at all times, we must be willing to be universally creative. The willingness is what counts. Do we accept that we as human beings have it in us to turn all things to the good? The 'how' will always occur to us at whatever particular time and we do not concern ourselves over it ahead of time. The 'that' is up to us.

*

No one is able to see light as such. At the same time, when we see beings we may know that our judicious awareness of beings brings this light to the fore so that beings are, as it were, illumined from within (compared to things, which are merely external) whereupon we ourselves stand revealed to ourselves as similarly illumined from within. We worship in reality.

36

Calling light an ordinant of our awareness is a little bit, but only a little bit, like wishful thinking because no evidence of light as information will persuade us of any logic in its value as an ordinant. An ordinant prevails when we stray off the mark, which happens so readily. That is why I say that we must be taught the value of light as an ordinant and that only practice will engrain this notion of it until it becomes a good habit and all our seeing, our sensing, will then be informed by light.

I say that we tend to stray off the mark but let's keep in mind that the so-called mark here is illumined seeing itself. I repeatedly speak of seeing because we naturally associate light with seeing and because this sense is my main one. I could as readily speak of sensing, and as we know, sometimes hearing is the prevalent sense, or even touching and feeling. In fact, 'light' could readily be associated in our minds with all our senses. An illumined existence is not limited to experience of the eye.

*

In any case, I cannot see why we should not say 'awareness' instead of 'sensation plus light'. Furthermore, since our body is not only sensation, or sense, but also feeling and emotion, we really need to include these too when we identify the information of light. And since body is distinct from mind only when and while we work towards its unification with mind, we can arrive at the conclusion that our body is informed by light just as our mind is guided by *the* light.

* * *

(August 2007)